JEWISH HOLIDAY ORIGAMI

JEWISH HOLIDAY ORIGAMI

Joel Stern

Photographs by
David Greenfield

Dover Publications, Inc.
Mineola, New York

Dedication

To my children Rena, Ethan, and Anna, who occasionally allow me to teach them a thing or two.

Acknowledgements

This book could not have been produced without the help of the following people:

To Florence Temko for your counsel and friendship, and for blazing so many origami trails, including the Jewish one.

To Boaz Shuval for your rigorous and insightful edits of the diagrams.

To David Greenfield for the beautiful photographs of the models.

To Hallie Lerman for generously sharing your time and expertise.

To Harry Chiel, Willie Inchinaga, Leslie Lawson, Greg Long, and Jim Stern for test-folding the models and for your constructive suggestions.

To Ariel Albornoz, Bennett Arnstein, Dorothy Engleman, Gil Graff, Karen Graham, Gay Merrill Gross, Sharon Hearn, Robert Lang, John Montroll, Edmon Rodman, Ellen Rubin, Lisa Silverman, Jessica Teich, Ken Tucker, and Abigail Yasgur for your support and advice along the way.

To Norman and Lela Jacoby, and Bates and Petty Metson for your ongoing love and encouragement.

To my sister Nancy Laub for teaching me my first origami.

To my wife Susan for everything.

Copyright

Copyright © 2006 by Joel Stern
All rights reserved.

Bibliographical Note

Jewish Holiday Origami is a new work, first published by
Dover Publications, Inc., in 2006.

Library of Congress Cataloging-in-Publication Data

Stern, Joel, 1953–
 Jewish holiday origami / Joel Stern.
  p. cm.
 ISBN-13: 978-0-486-45076-6 (pbk.)
 ISBN-10: 0-486-45076-7 (pbk.)
  1. Origami. 2. Holiday decorations. 3. Jewish crafts. 4. Fasts and feasts—Judaism. I. Title.

TT870.S727 2006
736'.982—dc22

2005056934

Manufactured in the United States by Courier Corporation
45076705
www.doverpublications.com

Table of Contents

Introduction

What is Origami?

Origami, a word of Japanese origin, is the art of folding paper. It is both an ancient and a very new art—many models have been around for hundreds of years, while new ones are being created all the time. Origami paper is usually colored on one side and white on the other. Most people who do origami follow these rules: You must start with a square, and you must not cut the paper. Yet despite these restrictions, there is no limit to what can be represented using origami—objects, people, plants, animals, even mountains and seas.

What is Jewish Origami?

Origami and Judaism? At first, you might not think that the two are related. In fact, not only are they related, but origami can even enhance your experience of Judaism, and vice versa. Here are some examples:

A *mitzvah* in Judaism is something we are obligated to do, such as lighting Chanukah candles. If we go beyond the obligation by making the experience more beautiful, such as when we use an especially attractive Chanukah menorah, we are following the principle of *hiddur mitzvah*, or enhancing of the mitzvah. When you make origami to decorate your holiday tables to make them more festive, you are following the principle of hiddur mitzvah.

In Judaism, you'll find many stories that fill in the gaps between the episodes in the Bible. These stories are called *midrashim*, and they often emphasize a particular aspect of a biblical character's personality. Origami is like a midrash—it emphasizes a particular aspect of a subject. For example, paperfolders around the world have created many different kinds of origami elephants, each emphasizing a different feature of the animal. Some highlight the animal's trunk, others its tusks, while others focus on its big floppy ears. When you create an origami model, you are, in a way, making a midrash about your subject.

Akira Yoshizawa was a Japanese origami master who devoted his life to studying nature, and creating origami models of what he observed. He noticed how plants grew and how animals moved, and the models he created are filled with life. Among other things, Yoshizawa taught that we should have great respect for nature. Judaism, too, teaches us to respect nature. For example, according to the Torah, we should let the land rest one year out of every seven, and on the holiday of Tu B'Shvat we are encouraged to plant trees and enjoy their fruits. When you have appreciation for nature, you not only honor Judaism, you also put yourself in the best frame of mind for doing origami.

How this Book is Organized

The models appear in the book by level of experience required, from beginner to advanced. The Table of Contents lists them in this order, as well as by order of Jewish holiday. In the Additional Resources section at the back you'll find books and Web sites for more models, sources for origami paper, and origami organizations.

Tips for Success

The folding sequences are broken down into small steps so that you'll be able to follow along, even if you've never done origami before. Make sure you review the diagramming symbols described on the next page. Fold patiently and accurately, always checking the next step to see the result of the move. Fold the beginner models first, then try your hand at the intermediate and advanced ones. The main thing is not to be discouraged. If your results don't match the picture, set the model aside and try again later. With each attempt, you'll get closer to the goal.

Have Fun!

I hope you have as much fun folding the models in this book as I had creating them. Feel free to change them as you like, or even create your own!

Symbols

The origami symbols used in this book are standard throughout the world. You'll find that as you become accustomed to working with them, you'll be able to read the diagrams without referring to the words.

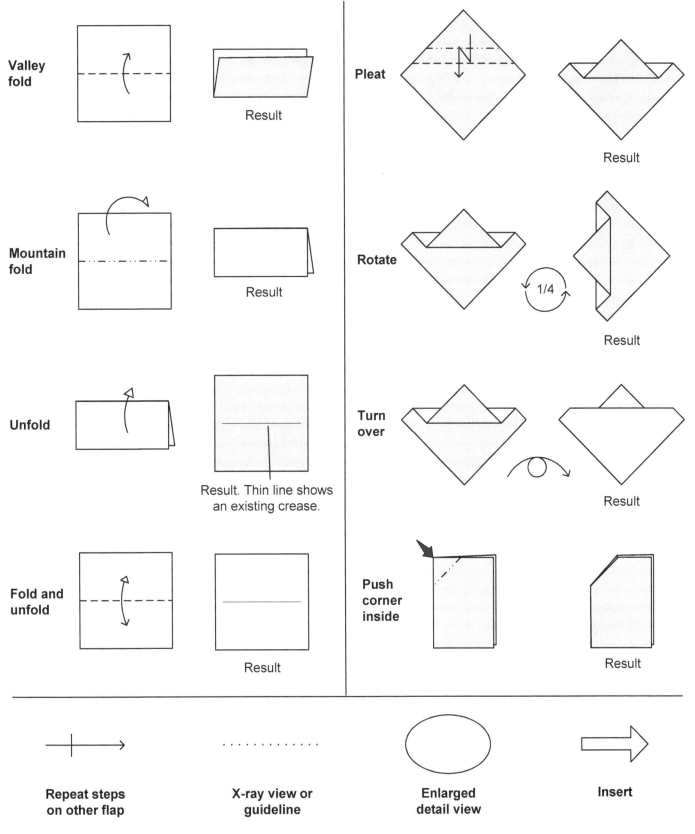

Valley fold — Result

Mountain fold — Result

Unfold — Result. Thin line shows an existing crease.

Fold and unfold — Result

Pleat — Result

Rotate — 1/4 — Result

Turn over — Result

Push corner inside — Result

Repeat steps on other flap

X-ray view or guideline

Enlarged detail view

Insert

Shofar (Ram's Horn)

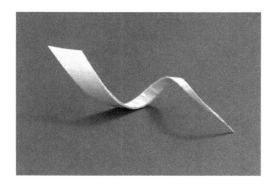

The "shofar," an ancient wind instrument made from a ram's horn, is sounded daily the last month of the Jewish year and during Rosh Hashanah, the New Year. One of the reasons it is blown during this season is to awaken us to examine our deeds so that we can learn to be better people.

The shofar comes in two shapes—straight (with a slight curve at the end), and spiral. The spiral kind, modeled here, is known as a Yemenite shofar because it was first used by the Jews of Yemen.

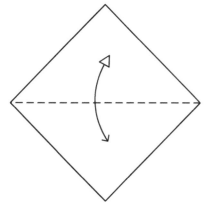

1. Begin with the white side up. Valley-fold and unfold the model diagonally.

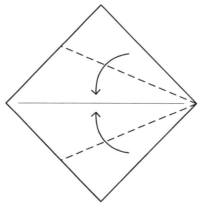

2. Valley-fold the two edges on the right to the crease made in step 1. Leave a gap in the center so that you'll be able to fold the model in half in step 5.

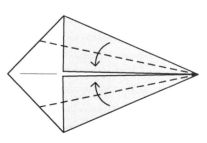

3. Again, valley-fold the two edges on the right to the crease made in step 1, leaving a gap.

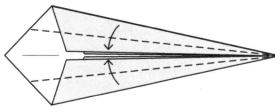

4. For the last time, valley-fold the edges on the right to the center, still leaving a gap.

5. Valley-fold the model in half along the diagonal.

Here is the result.

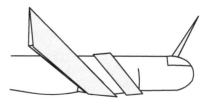

6. Wrap the model around your finger a few times; then remove your finger. Continue shaping the model as desired.

The Shofar

Siddur (Prayer Book)

The Hebrew word "siddur," or prayer book, actually means "order," and refers to the order of prayers in the service. The prayers in the siddur were composed over many centuries, and embody the thoughts, hopes, and dreams of the Jewish people.

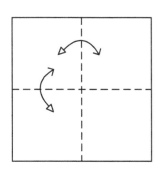

1. Begin with the white side up. Valley-fold and unfold the model in half in both directions.

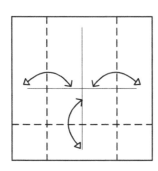

2. Valley-fold and unfold three sides to the creases made in step 1.

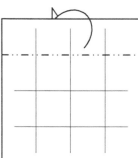

3. Mountain-fold the top edge to the center crease.

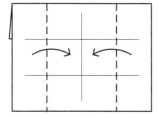

4. Valley-fold the two sides to the middle.

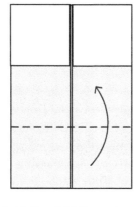

5. Valley-fold the colored portion in half.

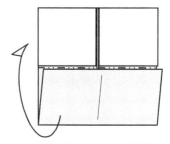

6. Mountain-fold the colored portion behind.

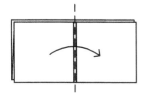

7. Valley-fold the model in half.

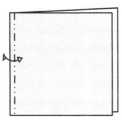

8. To create the impression that the book has a spine, mountain-fold and unfold the left edge a little bit along the crease line indicated.

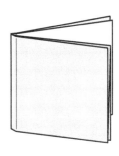

The Siddur

Sabbath Candles

The two candles we light just before the Sabbath represent the two commandments in the Torah that tell us to "remember" and "keep" the Sabbath. Some families have a tradition of lighting additional candles for each child or member of the household.

Use paper that is the color of fire — either yellow or orange.

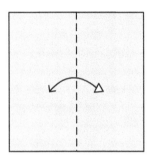

1. Begin with the color side up. Valley-fold and unfold the model side to side.

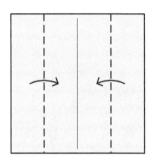

2. Valley-fold both sides to the center.

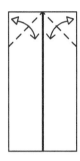

3. Valley-fold and unfold the two upper corners to the center.

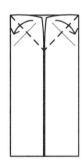

4. Valley-fold the inside top corners outward to lie along the right and left sides.

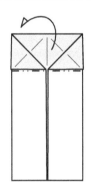

5. Mountain-fold the colored portion of the model behind.

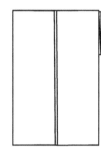

6. Turn the model over.

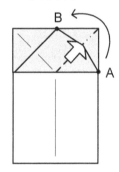

7. Insert your finger into the pocket of the flap at the right, lifting and moving point A to meet point B; then squash.

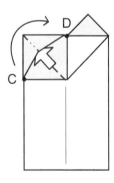

8. Repeat step 7 on the left side, lifting point C to meet point D.

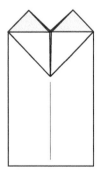

9. Turn the model over.

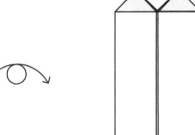

The Sabbath Candles

Tablets of the Ten Commandments

Seven weeks after Passover, we commemorate the giving of the Ten Commandments on Mt. Sinai with the festival of Shavuot. This is a model of the two stone tablets on which, we are told, the Ten Commandments were engraved.

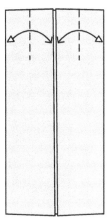

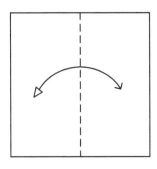

1. Begin with the white side facing you. Valley-fold the left side to the right, then unfold.

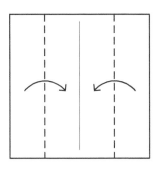

2. Valley-fold both left and right edges to the center crease.

3. At the top, pinch the half-way points between the center and outside edges.

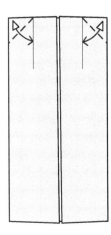

4. Valley-fold the top outside corners so the top edges lie along the creases you made in step 3, then unfold.

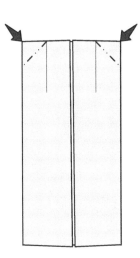

5. Push the corners inside along the creases made in step 4.

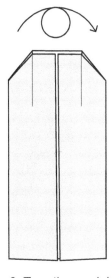

6. Turn the model over.

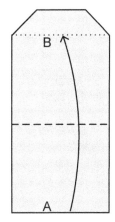

7. Valley-fold the bottom edge A to the base of the trapezoidal shape at B, as indicated by the dotted line.

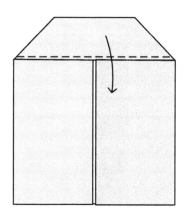

8. Valley-fold the top layer down on top of the lower flap.

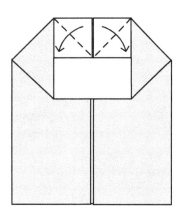

9. Valley-fold the two white corners at the top down diagonally.

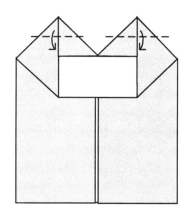

10. Valley-fold both tips down to the top corners of the white rectangle.

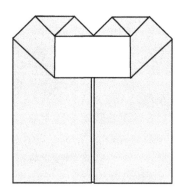

11. Turn the model over.

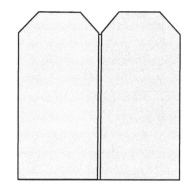

The Tablets of the Ten Commandments

Ushpiz (Sukkot Guest)

While wandering in the desert after leaving Egypt, the Jews lived in small huts called "sukkot." This experience is commemorated today in the seven-day festival of Sukkot, during which time Jews dwell in their own sukkot, inviting the spirits of seven Biblical ancestors as guests, or "ushpizin," each night. These guests are Abraham, Isaac, Jacob, Moses, Joseph, Aaron, and David.

You can also welcome the spirits of seven women from Jewish history during this festival. One of them is Miriam, Moses' sister, and you'll find an origami version of her on page 22.

You can alter a number of features of this model to make different-looking ushpizin – a longer beard, a wider hood, etc.

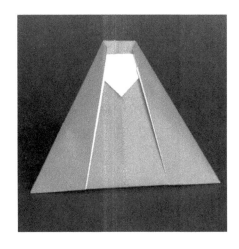

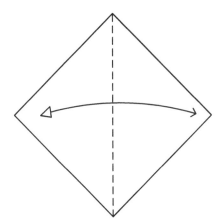

1. Begin with the white side up. Valley-fold the left corner to the right, then unfold.

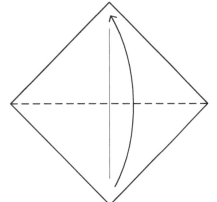

2. Valley-fold the bottom corner to the top.

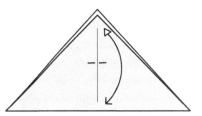

3. Steps 3-4 are on the top layer only. Valley-fold the top point to the bottom and make a pinch. Then unfold.

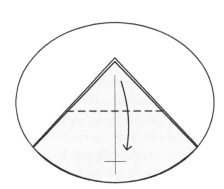

4. Valley-fold the top point to the crease made in step 3.

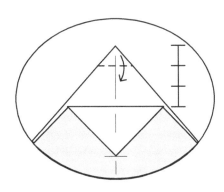

5. Valley-fold the tip of the bottom layer about 1/3 of the distance to the edge of the top layer.

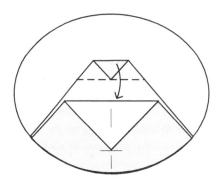

6. Valley-fold the top edge of the bottom layer to meet the top edge of the bottom layer.

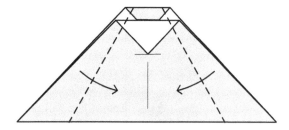

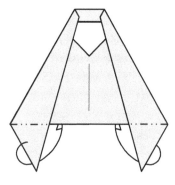

7. Valley-fold the model inward from the left and right to form the hood. There are no landmarks for where to put these creases. The farther in you fold the edges, the larger the hood.

8. Mountain-fold to the rear the portion of the flaps that extend beyond the base of the figure. Do not fold them all the way back, only enough to prop the model up.

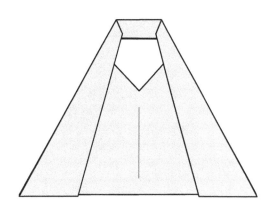

The Sukkot Guest

A view from the side

Pyramid

The pyramids remind us of the harsh conditions under which the Jewish slaves were forced to work in ancient Egypt. During the Passover Seder we eat a special food called "charoset," a mixture of nuts, wine, apples, and cinnamon that represents the mortar that held the bricks of the pyramid together.

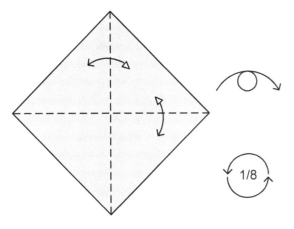

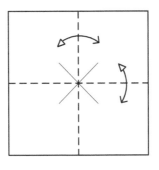

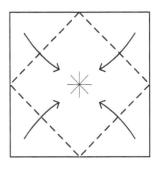

1. Begin with the colored side up. Valley-fold and unfold diagonally in both directions. Rotate the model 1/8 of a turn and turn it over.

2. Valley-fold and unfold side to side in both directions.

3. Valley-fold all four corners to the center.

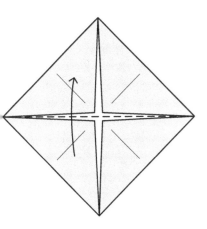

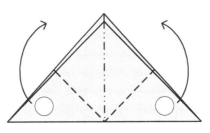

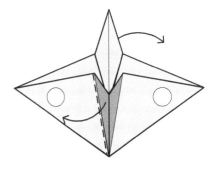

4. Valley-fold bottom to top.

5. Grasp the model at the circles and swing the corners up and inside. As you do this, flaps will emerge from the center of the model in front and in back.

6. Once the flaps are pointing front and back, swivel the front flap to the left and the back flap to the right.

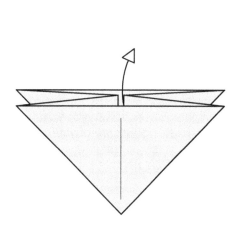

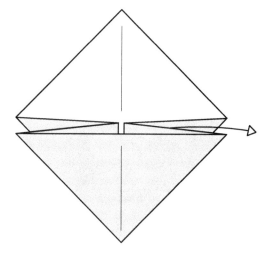

7. Unfold the single corner flap stuck inside at the back.

8. Pull open the flap at the right.

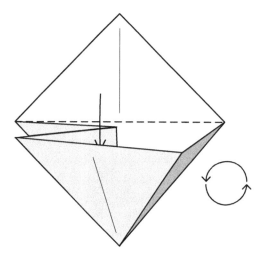

9. Valley-fold the corner flap back inside, folding it over the doubled flap on the left. Then turn the model over and spread it open.

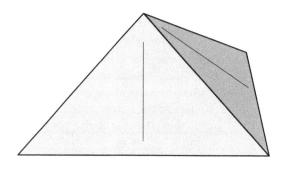

The Pyramid

Dreidel

The "dreidel" is a traditional Chanukah spinning toy. The four Hebrew letters that appear on its sides – nun, gimmel, hey, shin – stand for the Hebrew words "Nes Gadol Hayah Sham" - "A great miracle happened there." This refers to the miraculous victory of the few Maccabees over the might of the Greek Empire. In Israel, instead of the letter "shin" they use the letter "peh," which stands for "Poh." "Poh" means "here," which indicates that a great miracle happened <u>here</u>, not <u>there</u>.

Our origami dreidel is made from two identically folded sheets of different colors.

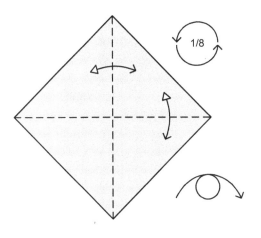

1. Begin with the color side up. Valley-fold the left corner to the right and unfold. Valley-fold the top corner to the bottom and unfold. Rotate 1/8 and turn over.

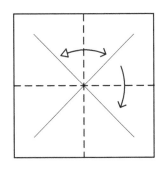

2. Valley-fold left side to right and unfold. Valley-fold the top to the bottom.

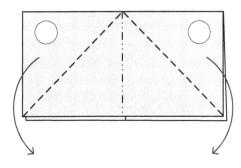

3. Grasp the model at the circles and swing the lower corners down and together. As you do this, flaps will emerge from the center of the model in front and back.

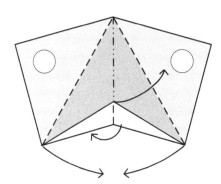

Step 3 in progress

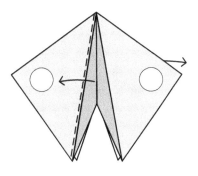

4. Swivel the front flap to the left, and the rear flap to the right. Then lay the model flat.

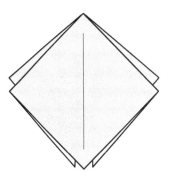

5. Half the dreidel is complete. Make another piece using a different color.

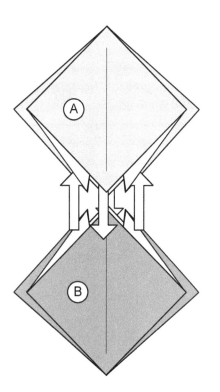

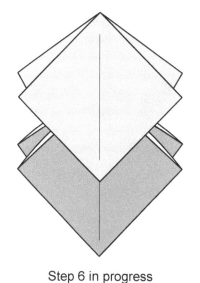

Step 6 in progress

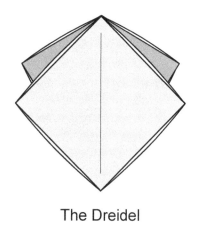

The Dreidel

6. Feed the two pieces together, laying the front and back flaps of piece A on top, and the inside right and left flaps of piece B on top. When finished, the model will have sides of alternating colors.

Write the four Hebrew letters as shown below on the dreidel, one on each of the four faces.

To play, first distribute an equal number of tokens (pennies, nuts, chocolate coins, etc.) to each player. The player holds the model as shown, spins it, and does what the letter that ends up on top says to do, based on the key below. Then the dreidel passes to the next player.

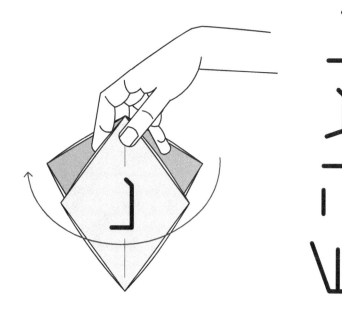

Nun – Nothing happens.

Gimmel – Take everything in the pot.

Hey – Take half the pot.

Shin – Put one token into the pot.

Hamentash (Purim Pastry)

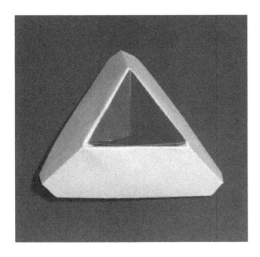

A "hamentash" is a traditional three-cornered Purim pastry. Some people think its shape represents the hat of Haman, the villain of the Purim story. In Israel it's called "Ozen Haman," or "Haman's ear." Typical fillings for hamentashen are poppy seeds, prunes, apricots, or chocolate chips.

This model has two pieces – the hamentash and the filling. Both pieces begin with pyramids of different sizes. It's fun to think that, at least with origami, one can change a pyramid, a symbol of tyranny and ruthless power, into a hamentash, a symbol of sweetness and joy, with just a few creases.

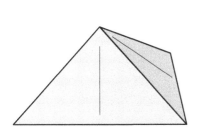

1. Begin with the Pyramid, page 13.

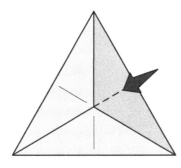

2. Top view. Push in at the valley-fold crease on the side. The model will begin to flatten.

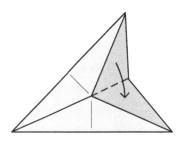

3. Continue flattening.

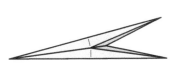

4. Flattening completed. Turn the model back to the upright position.

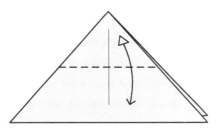

5. Valley-fold and unfold the model in half, top to bottom.

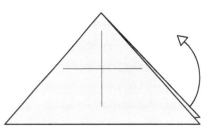

6. Open up the model to the position in step 1.

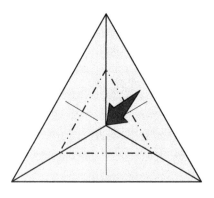

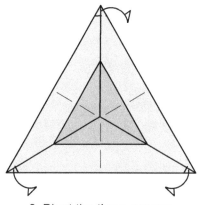

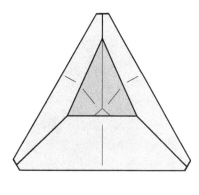

7. Top view. Press the top of the model inside along the crease lines you made in step 6, creating a hollowed-out pyramid shape.

8. Blunt the three corners with mountain folds.

The Hamentash

Filling

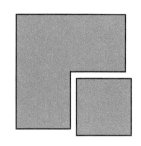

Make the filling from a piece of paper 1/4 the size of the one used to make the hamentash.

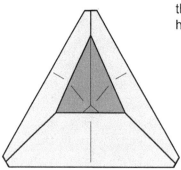

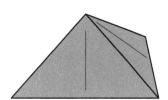

1. Make a pyramid, page 13, and turn it upside-down.

2. Insert the pyramid snugly into the cavity on the top of the hamentash.

The Hamentash
with Filling

Kiddush Cup

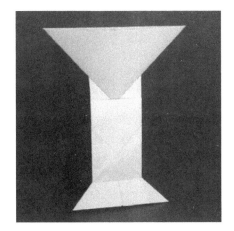

In Judaism, wine is used to help celebrate holy days, like the Sabbath and holidays, as well as special moments in our lives, like weddings. At these times, we drink the wine from a special goblet called a "kiddush cup," after reciting a blessing. One custom is to let the cup overflow a bit to show our gratitude for life's blessings.

This model has two parts – a stem and a bowl.

Stem

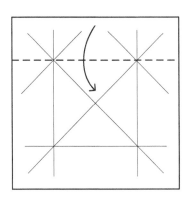

1. Begin with the white side up. Valley-fold and unfold diagonally in both directions. Then rotate it 1/8 of a turn.

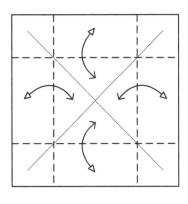

2. Valley-fold and unfold all four sides to the center.

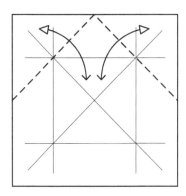

3. Valley-fold and unfold the top right and left corners to the center.

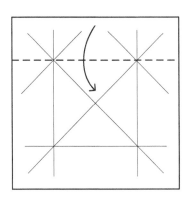

4. Valley-fold the top edge to the center, using the existing crease.

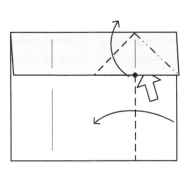

5. Lift the top flap at the dot, while at the same time swinging the right edge to the center.

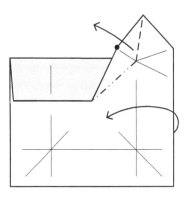

Step 5 in progress

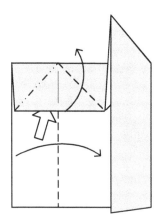
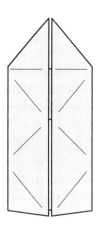
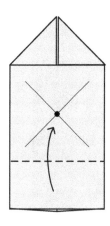

7. The right flap is complete. Repeat steps 5-6 on the left side.

8. Turn the model over.

9. Valley-fold the bottom edge to the center (indicated by a dot), along the existing crease.

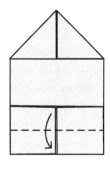
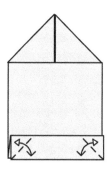
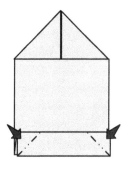

10. Valley-fold the top of the flap down to the bottom edge.

11. Valley-fold and unfold the two corners at 45°.

12. Push in the two corners along the creases.

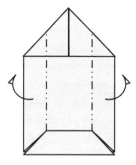
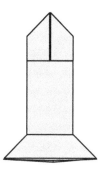

13. Mountain-fold the right and left sides of the model behind, except for the two triangular flaps at the bottom.

The Kiddush Cup Stem

Bowl

Begin with steps 1-6 of the Pyramid, page 13.

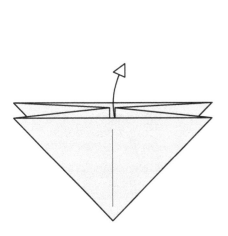

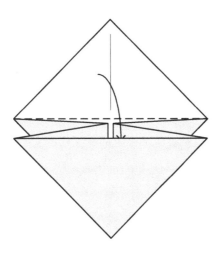

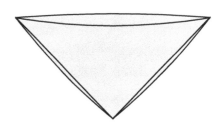

1. Unfold the single corner flap stuck inside at the back.

2. Valley-fold the corner flap back inside, folding it over both doubled flaps.

The Kiddush Cup Bowl

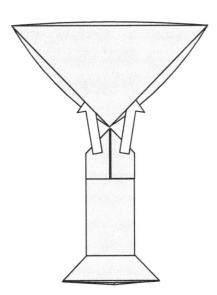

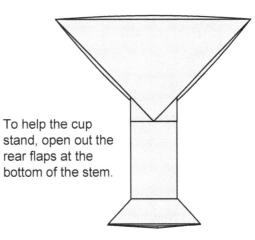

Join the two parts by inserting the pointed flaps at the top of the stem into the slots on the bottom of the bowl. You can use glue, if you like, to keep the model secure.

To help the cup stand, open out the rear flaps at the bottom of the stem.

The Kiddush Cup

21

Miriam with Timbrel

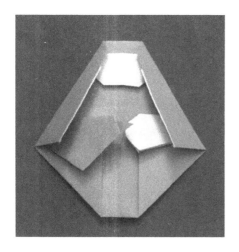

On the holiday of Sukkot there is a tradition to invite the spirits of seven men from the Bible, called "ushpizin," to our festive meals. (See page 11 for an origami ushpiz.) In addition to the men, we can also welcome the spirits of seven women from Jewish history. One of these is Moses' sister Miriam who, the Torah tells us, played her timbrel (or drum) in celebration after the Jews crossed the Red Sea. Isn't it surprising that, despite the great haste in which she left Egypt, Miriam still took the time to pack a musical instrument? Miriam's action teaches us that despite life's hardships, one should always seek out and prepare for moments of celebration.

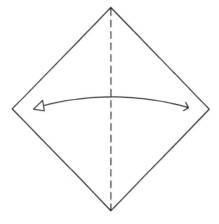

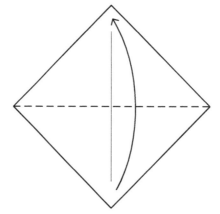

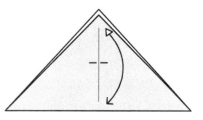

1. Begin with the white side up. Valley-fold the left corner to the right, then unfold.

2. Valley-fold the bottom corner to the top.

3. Steps 3-5 are done on the top layer only. Valley-fold the top point to the bottom and make a pinch. Then unfold.

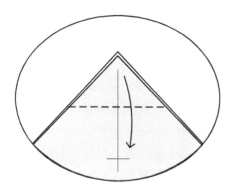

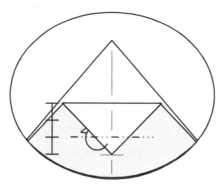

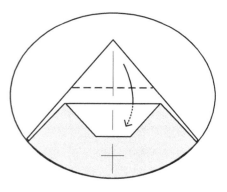

4. Valley-fold the top point to the pinch mark made in step 3.

5. Mountain-fold the tip of the white triangle under about 1/3 of the distance from the tip to the inside top edge. There are no landmarks.

6. Valley-fold the tip of the remaining flap down and tuck it under the top layer. Again, there are no landmarks, but the resulting colored top stripe should be about half the height of the white trapezoid.

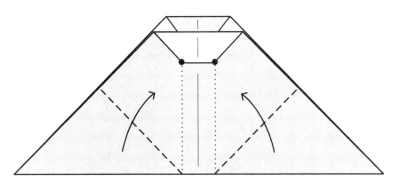

7. Valley-fold the two corners up so that the bottom edges lie along the dotted lines, and pass through the bottom corners of the white trapezoid (marked with dots).

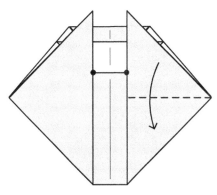

8. Valley-fold the right flap down in half.

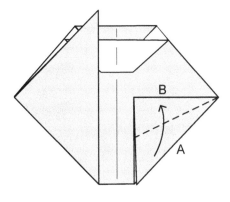

9. Valley-fold the right flap up so that edge A meets edge B.

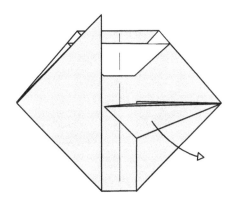

10. On the right flap, undo steps 7, 8, and 9.

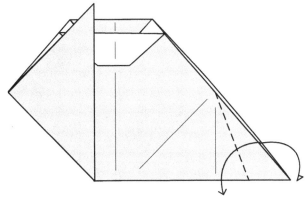

11. Wrap the right flap inside-out along the crease nearest the right edge (the one you made in step 9), revealing the white side. You may have to open up the model to do this.

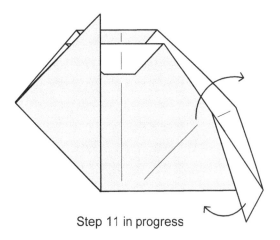

Step 11 in progress

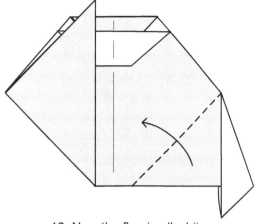

12. Now the flap is all white and will be shaped to form the timbrel. Restore the valley-fold from step 7.

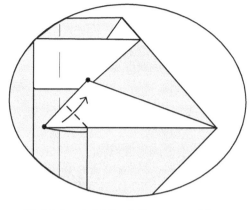

13. Valley-fold the left corner of the timbrel flap up and to the right, connecting the two dots.

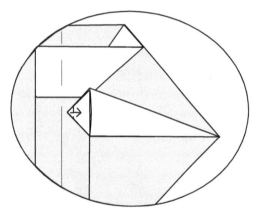

14. Valley-fold the tip of the timbrel flap directly to the right. There is no landmark for this crease.

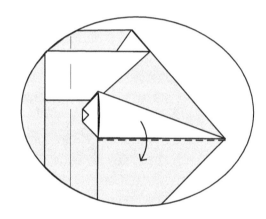

15. Valley-fold the timbrel flap down along the existing crease.

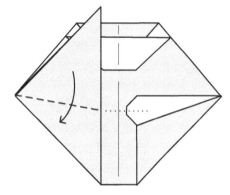

16. Valley-fold the left flap down and to the left, beginning from the left corner to a point directly across from the middle of the right flap (indicated with a dotted line). This will form the arm.

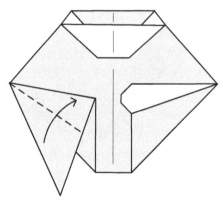

17. Valley-fold the arm flap up and to the right, so that it overlaps the timbrel flap.

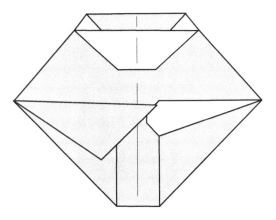

Result of step 17

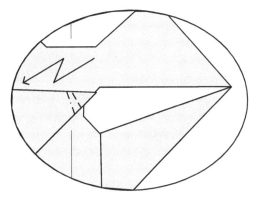

18. This shows a close-up of the hand. Pleat the tip of the arm flap with a mountain- and valley-fold to form a hand. There are no landmarks for this move.

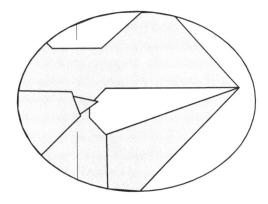

Result of step 18

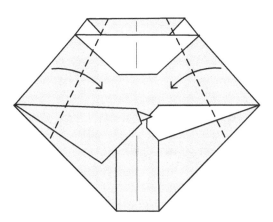

19. Valley-fold the entire model on the left and right to form the sides of Miriam's hood. You can make the hood as wide or narrow as you like.

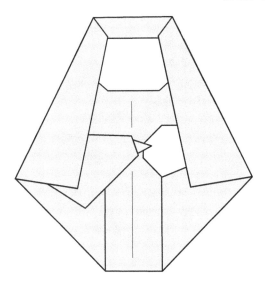

Miriam with Timbrel

Menorah with Candles

A nine-branched candelabra, called a "menorah," is lit each evening of the eight-day festival of Chanukah, with one candle added each night, and one, called the "shammash" or "helper," to light the others. The candles recall the miracle of the lamp, discovered in the ruined Temple, which contained only enough oil to burn for one day, but instead burned for eight.

This model has two parts – the menorah itself and the candles. A triangular flap extends above the candles to indicate the shammash.

For the menorah, use silver or gold foil-backed paper. For the candles, use paper the color of fire – either yellow or orange.

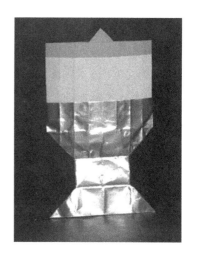

Menorah

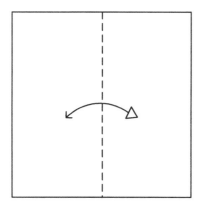

1. Begin with the white side up. Valley-fold and unfold the model side to side.

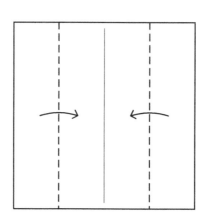

2. Valley-fold both sides to the center.

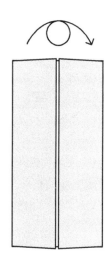

3. Turn the model over.

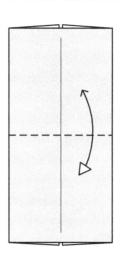

4. Valley-fold and unfold the bottom edge to the top.

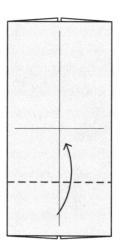

5. Valley-fold the bottom edge to the crease you made in the previous step.

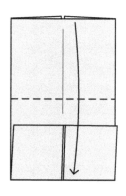

6. Valley-fold the top edge to the bottom edge.

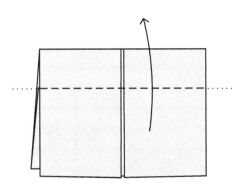

7. Valley-fold the bottom edge up, making a crease that lies along the top edge of the underlying flap (shown with a dotted line).

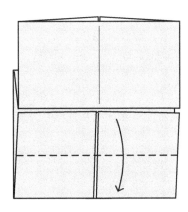

8. Valley-fold the top edge of the lower flap to lie along the bottom.

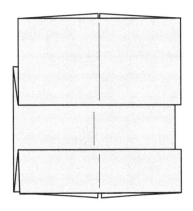

9. Turn the model over.

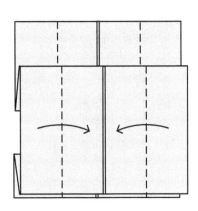

10. Valley-fold the two sides to the center through all thicknesses.

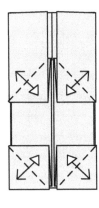

11. Valley-fold the four inside corners outward at 45°. Then unfold.

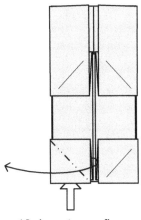

12. Insert your finger under the square flap at the lower left, and open it to the left. When it becomes triangular, squash it flat.

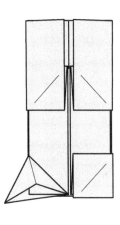

Step 12 in progress

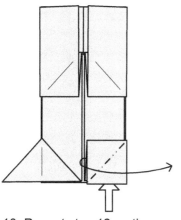 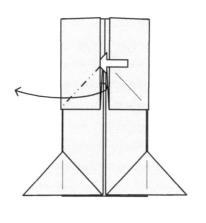 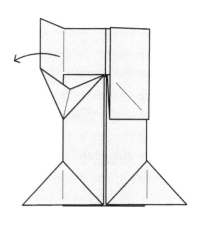

13. Repeat step 12 on the lower right flap.

14. Do the same move on the upper left flap.

Step 14 in progress

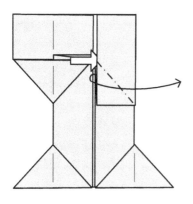 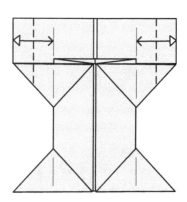

15. Repeat step 14 on the upper right flap.

16. Valley-fold and unfold the left and right edges to the creases indicated.

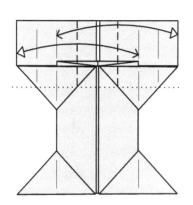 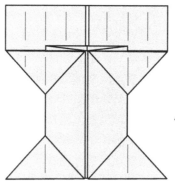 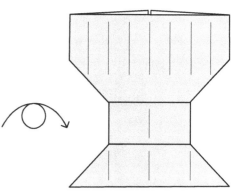

17. Valley-fold and unfold the left and right edges to the same creases as in step 16, but on the opposite side of the model. Only crease down as far as the dotted line.

17. The result is that the top of the menorah will be divided into eight sections. Turn the model over.

The Menorah

Menorah Candles

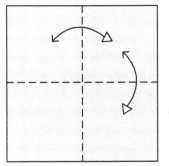 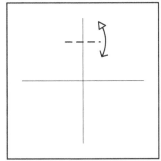

1. Begin with the color side up. Valley-fold and unfold the model side to side in both directions. Then turn the model over.

2. Pinch the half-way point between the top edge and the center.

3. Pinch the half-way point between the edge and the pinch mark you made in step 2.

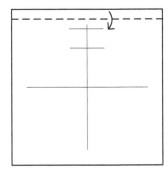 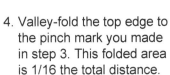 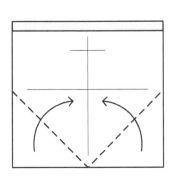 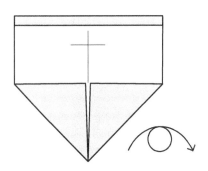

4. Valley-fold the top edge to the pinch mark you made in step 3. This folded area is 1/16 the total distance.

5. Valley-fold both lower corners to the center.

6. Turn the model over.

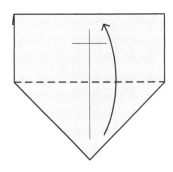 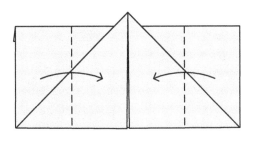 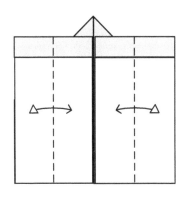

7. Valley-fold the model up at the widest part of the triangular area. The tip will stick out over the top.

8. Valley-fold both sides to the center.

9. Valley-fold and unfold both sides to the center.

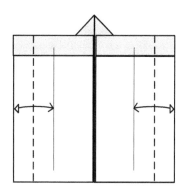

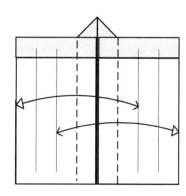

10. Valley-fold and unfold the left and right edges to the creases you made in step 9.

11. Valley-fold and unfold the left and right edges to the same creases as in step 10, but on the opposite side of the model. This makes eight "candles."

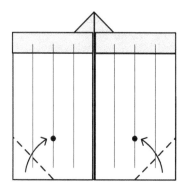

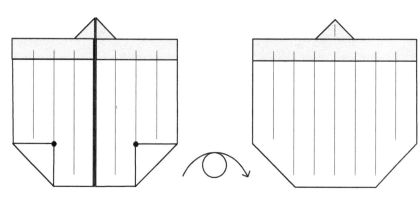

11. Valley-fold the lower left and right corners up at 45° to the dots (the second creases from the right and left).

12. Turn the model over.

The Menorah Candles

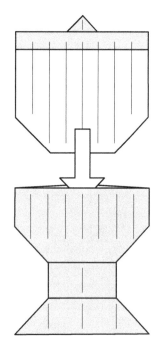

Insert the candles between the front and back flaps of the menorah.

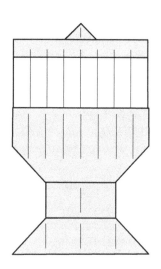

You can slide the candles down into the menorah to pretend they're burning.

The Menorah with Candles

Frog

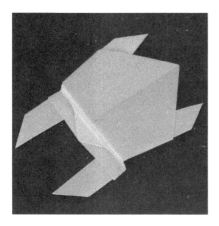

According to the Bible, the second of the Ten Plagues that God sent upon the Egyptians was frogs. This model jumps when you press its back, and will be a fun addition to your Passover Seder table.

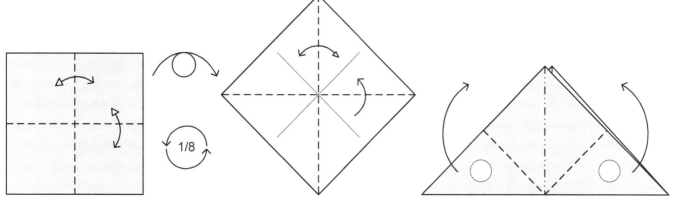

1. Begin with the color side up. Valley-fold and unfold side to side in both directions. Turn the model over and rotate it 1/8 of a turn.

2. Valley-fold and unfold the right corner to the left. Then valley-fold the bottom corner to the top.

3. Grasp the model at the circles and swing the corners up and inside. As you do this, flaps will emerge from the center of the model in front and in back.

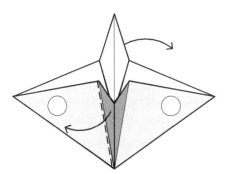

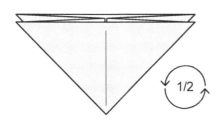

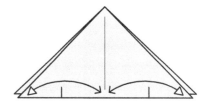

4. Once the flaps are pointing front and back, swivel the front flap to the left and the back flap to the right.

5. Rotate the model top to bottom.

6. Valley-fold the right and left corners to the center and pinch. Then unfold.

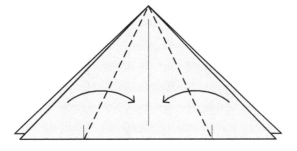

7. Make valley folds on the left and right front flaps that connect the top point with the pinch marks on the bottom edge.

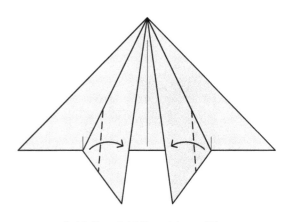

8. Valley-fold the sides of the front flaps in. There are no landmarks for these creases.

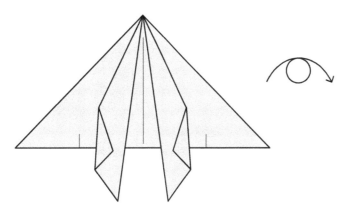

9. Turn the model over.

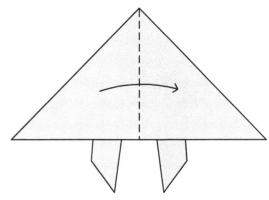

10. Valley-fold the left flap to the right along the center.

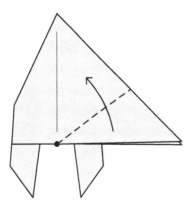

11. Valley-fold the right flap up and to the right, beginning at the mid-point of the base (shown with a dot). There is no landmark for the angle of this crease.

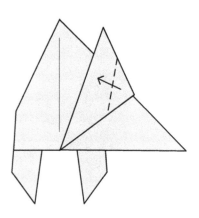

12. Valley-fold the right tip of the flap on the right over to the left. There are no landmarks.

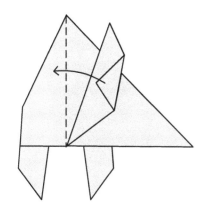

13. Return the flap structure on the right to its position in step 10.

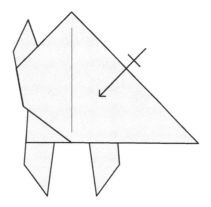

14. Repeat steps 10-13 on the flap on the right.

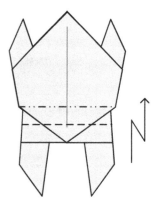

15. Pleat the body with a mountain- and valley-fold. This gives the model its "spring."

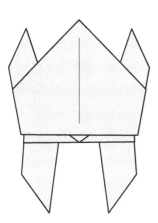

The Frog

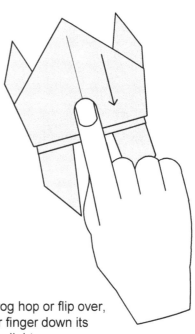

To make the frog hop or flip over, gently rub your finger down its back, applying slight pressure as you slide your finger off.

Shank Bone

The shank bone ("zeroah" in Hebrew), one of the objects on the Passover Seder plate, is a reminder of the lamb that was sacrificed the night of the exodus from Egypt. We might ask why the shank bone, or foreleg, was chosen as a reminder. One reason is that the word "zeroah" is the same word the Bible uses to describe God's outstretched arm when He took the Jews out of Egypt.

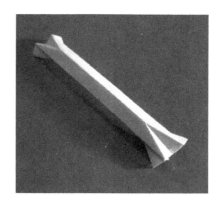

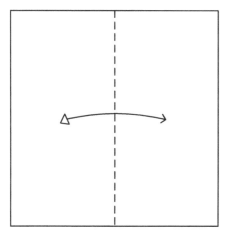

1. Begin with the white side up. Valley-fold left to right, then unfold.

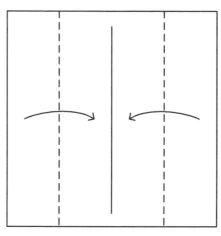

2. Valley-fold the left and right sides to the center. Try to leave a little gap in the center, because later on you'll need the room to accommodate the thickness of the paper.

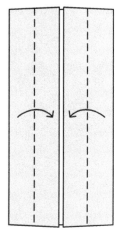

3. Valley-fold left and right sides to the center, again leaving a small gap.

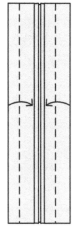

4. For the last time, valley-fold both sides to the center, again leaving a gap.

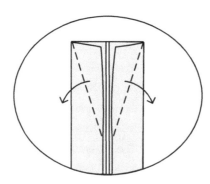

5. Valley-fold along diagonals connecting the outside corners to a point about 1/4 of the way down from the top. (It doesn't have to be exactly 1/4).

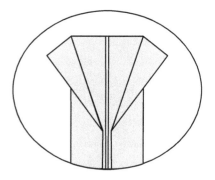

6. Here is the result. Repeat step 5 on the other end.

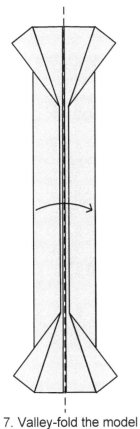

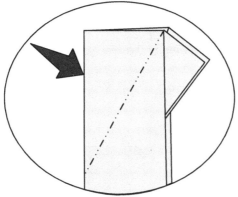

8. Push the corner inside from the left, so it's hidden inside the model.

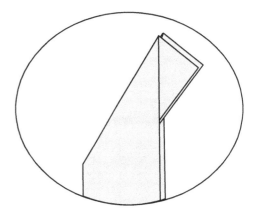

9. Here is the result. Repeat step 8 on the other end.

7. Valley-fold the model in half left to right.

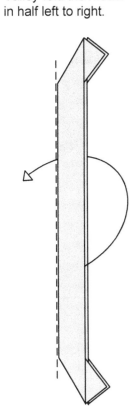

10. Unfold the model along the center, swinging the rear flap around to the left.

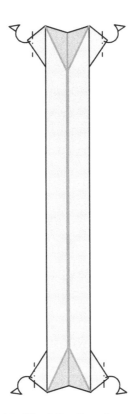

11. Blunt the four tips with mountain-folds.

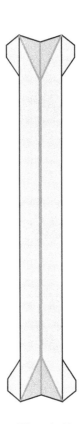

The Shank Bone

Chad Gadya (Kid)

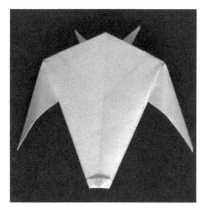

The last song of the Passover Seder is called "Chad Gadya," which means "one kid" or baby goat. In the song, father buys a kid for two "zuzim" or coins. The kid is eaten by a cat, who gets bitten by a dog, who is beaten by a stick, which is consumed by fire, and so on, until God finally ends the series of violent acts by destroying the Angel of Death. Some people interpret this song as a series of battles between nations, until, with the coming of the Messiah, all war will cease.

This model begins with steps 1-5 of the Frog, page 31.

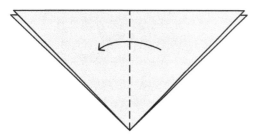

1. Valley-fold the right flap over to the left along the center.

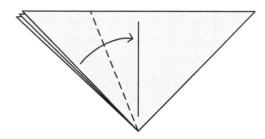

2. Valley-fold the left flap over so that the outside edge lies along the center.

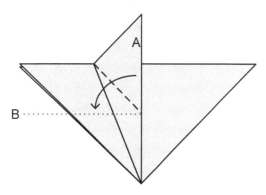

3. Valley-fold the left flap down and to the left so that edge A lies along an imaginary line B, which is parallel to the top of the model.

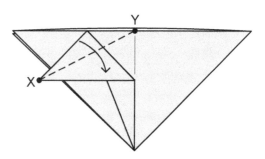

4. Valley-fold the flap structure along a line that connects its tip (X) to the midpoint of the top (Y).

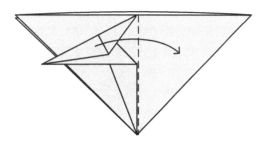

5. Valley-fold the entire flap structure over to the right along the center.

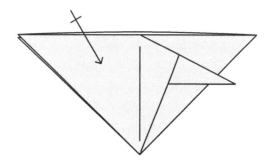

6. Repeat steps 1-5 on the left flap.

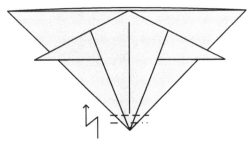

7. Pleat the bottom of the model with a valley- and mountain-fold to form the nose. There are no landmarks.

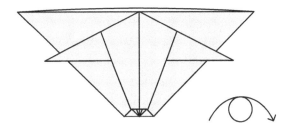

8. Turn the model over.

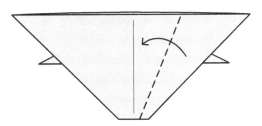

9. Valley-fold the flap on the right so that the right edge lies along the center.

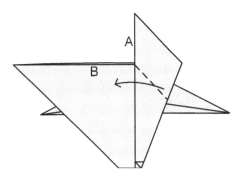

10. Valley-fold the flap on the right down and to the left so that the vertical edge A lies along horizontal edge B.

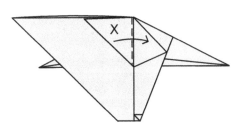

11. Valley-fold flap X to the right along the center.

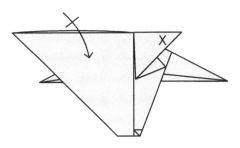

12. Repeat steps 9-11 on the left flap.

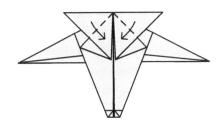

13. Valley-fold the two triangular flaps at the top so that the top edges lie along the center.

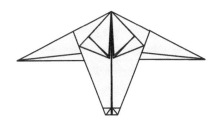

Here is the result. Continue with step 14.

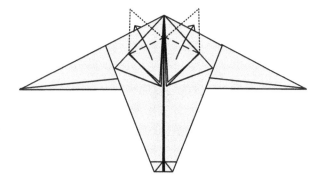

14. Valley-fold the indicated flaps up and out into the triangular dotted line areas, forming a diamond shape on either side.

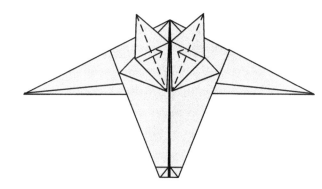

15. Valley-fold the same flaps, now shaped like diamonds, in half the long way.

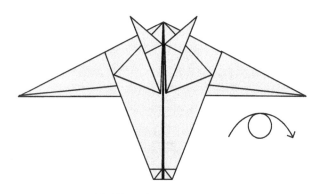

16. Turn the model over.

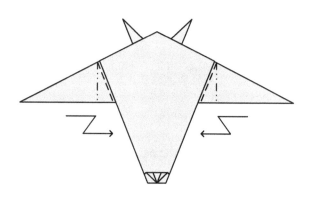

17. Pleat the ears and tuck them inside the head on both sides.

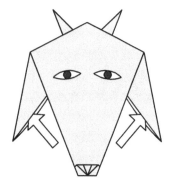

18. Open out the ears a bit. Draw eyes if you like.

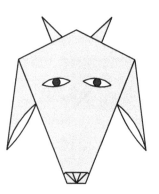

Chad Gadya

Two Zuzim (Coins)

The "Chad Gadya" song, which ends the Passover Seder, begins with the words: "One kid, one kid, that my father bought for two zuzim (coins)." In ancient times, two zuzim were equal to about two days' salary.

You can use this model to decorate your Seder table. For realistic-looking zuzim, use paper backed with silver or gold foil.

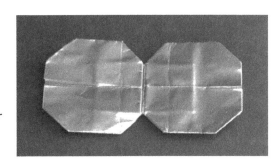

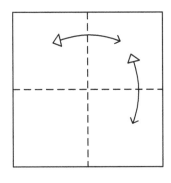

1. Begin with the white side up. Valley-fold side to side in both directions and unfold.

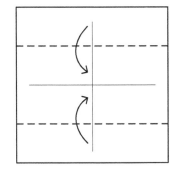

2. Valley-fold the top and bottom edges to the center.

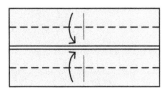

3. Valley-fold the top and bottom folded edges to the center.

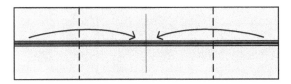

4. Valley-fold the left and right edges to the center.

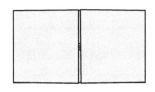

5. Turn the model over.

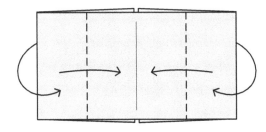

6. Valley-fold the left and right folded edges to the center, while letting the flaps underneath swing out and in front.

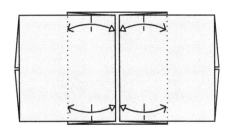

7. Valley-fold and unfold the inner edges outward to the dotted lines, but do not crease all the way. Just make pinch marks top and bottom.

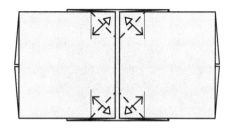

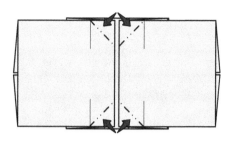

8. Valley-fold the four inside corners at 45° angles toward the pinch marks you made in step 7, then unfold them.

9. Push the four corners in to lie along the pinch marks you made in step 7.

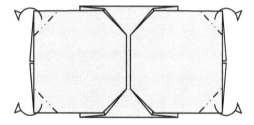

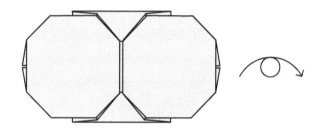

10. Mountain-fold the four outside corners behind. These corners should be the same size and at the same angle as the corners created in step 9. When you're done, you'll have two octagons.

11. Turn the model over.

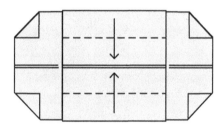

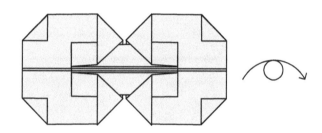

12. Valley-fold the uppermost layer of the center flap to the center, top and bottom. This makes the model fairly thick.

13. Turn the model over.

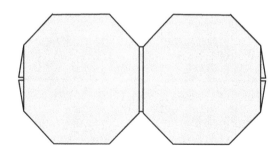

Two Zuzim

Red Sea Parting

There is a midrash, or legend, that the Red Sea didn't part right away when the Israelites approached it. It parted only after one man, Nachshon ben Aminadav, demonstrated his faith in God by plunging into the water.

This model lets you pretend you're Nachshon. Press down on the model along the central crease, creating a valley down the middle. Keeping your finger pressed, "walk" through the Red Sea. At the other side, lift your finger, allowing the model to spring back to its original position.

While you could use regular origami paper, I recommend using thicker paper, such as gift wrap, which will enhance the "spring" effect.

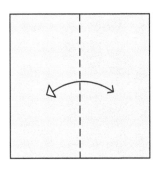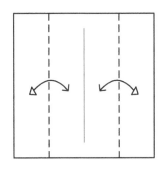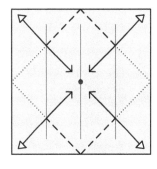

1. Begin with the color side up. Valley-fold and unfold left to right. Turn the model over.

2. Valley-fold and unfold both sides to the center. Turn the model over.

3. Valley-fold and unfold the four corners to the center (indicated with a black dot), but only to the creases made in step 2. (The dotted lines show where the folds would have continued.)

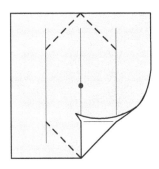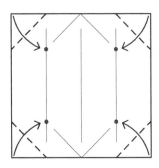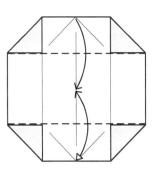

This drawing, which is in 3-D, shows this move on just the lower right corner. Once you've done this on all four corners, turn the model over.

4. Valley-fold the four corners to meet the creases made in step 2 (as indicated by the black dots).

5. Valley-fold the top and bottom edges to the center, keeping the corners tucked in. Unfold the bottom edge.

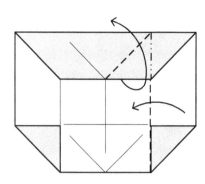

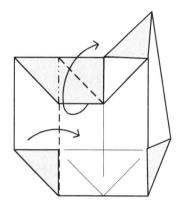

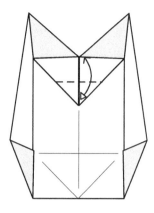

6. Lift up the colored flap along the diagonal valley-fold, while at the same time allowing the side to fold up at a 90° angle.

7. The model is now shown in 3-D. Repeat step 6 on the left side.

8. Valley-fold and unfold the tip of the triangle to its base.

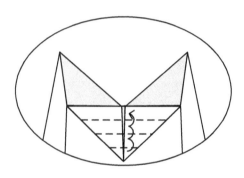

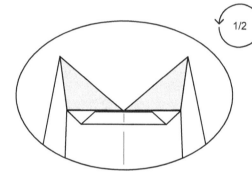

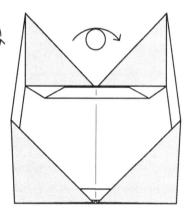

9. Fold up the triangular flap three times: the tip to the crease made in step 8, then along the crease from step 8, then again to the inside edge.

10. Step 9 completed. Rotate the model half way around, fold the other edge to the center, and repeat steps 6-9 on this flap. This will be a little more difficult because you'll have to work "inside the box."

11. Steps 6-9 are now completed on the other side. The model has two rectangular side walls, connected to triangular props in front and back. Flip the model over.

Press gently along the existing valley-fold. The model will collapse into two tent-like shapes.

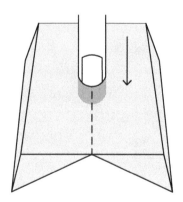

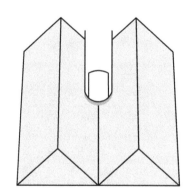

Walk your finger through. When you remove it, the model will spring back into its box-like shape.

Red Sea Parting

Four Sons

In the Haggadah, the book read during the Passover Seder that tells the story of the Exodus from Egypt, there is a passage that describes how one should teach the lessons of the holiday to Four Sons. Each of these sons exhibits a particular trait – wisdom, wickedness, simplicity, and innocence. In addition to acknowledging the uniqueness of each person, this passage demonstrates that everyone, regardless of background, ability, and attitude, is welcome at the Seder.

These four models, and a display stand, are diagrammed on the following pages.

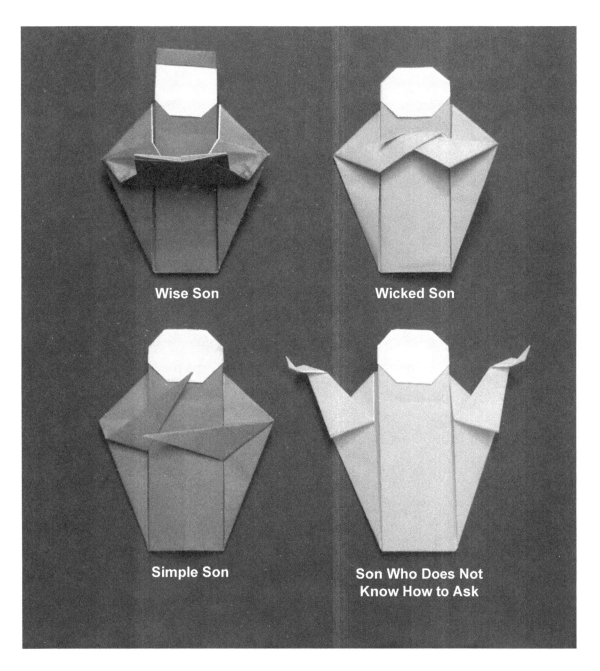

Wise Son

Wicked Son

Simple Son

Son Who Does Not Know How to Ask

Wise Son

In many Passover Haggadot, the Wise Son is portrayed as a scholar. I've chosen to show him praying, holding a siddur, which is made from a sheet 1/4 the size of that used for this model. (See page 7 for instructions on making a siddur.)

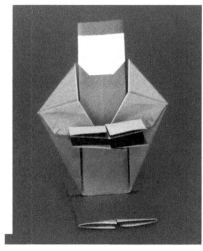

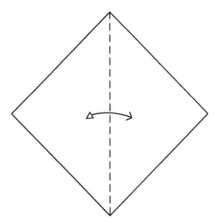

1. Begin with the white side up. Valley-fold left to right, then unfold.

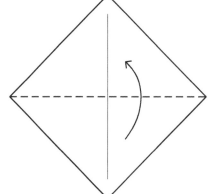

2. Valley-fold bottom to top.

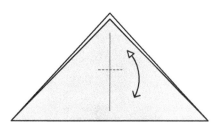

3. Steps 3-6 are on the top layer only. Valley-fold the top point to the bottom and make a pinch mark. Then unfold.

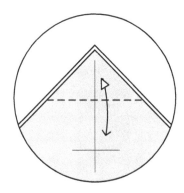

4. Valley-fold the top point to the crease made in step 3. Then unfold.

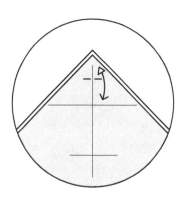

5. Valley-fold the top point down to the crease made in step 4 and make a short crease. Then unfold.

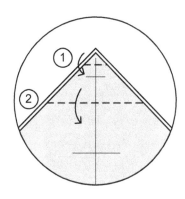

6. This step has two parts. First, valley-fold the top down to the crease made in step 5 (#1 on the diagram). Then re-fold the crease made in step 4 (#2 on the diagram).

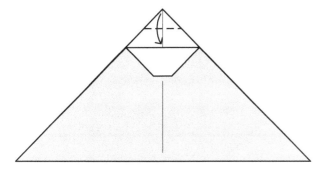

7. Valley-fold the top of the rear flap down to the top edge of the front flap.

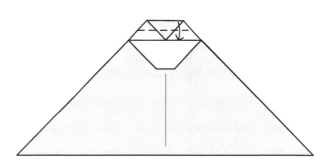

8. Valley-fold the top of the rear flap to lie along the top edge of the front flap.

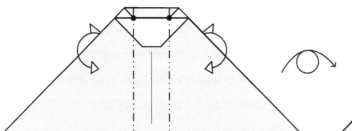

9. Make two vertical mountain-folds of the entire model at the points marked with the dots. Then unfold. Turn the model over.

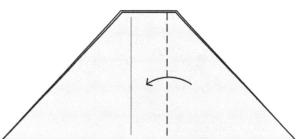

10. Valley-fold the right side over to the left along the crease made in step 9.

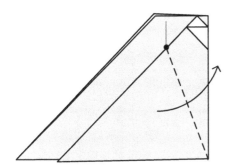

11. Valley-fold the flap, beginning at the lower-right corner and extending to a point that intersects with the vertical crease made in step 9 (indicated with a dot).

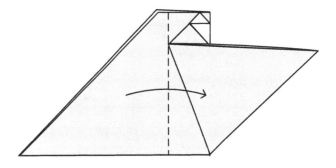

12. Valley-fold the left side over to the right along the crease made in step 9.

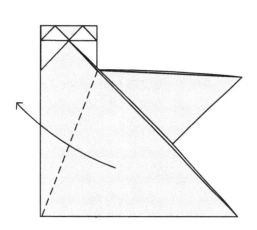

13. Valley fold the flap, beginning at the lower-left corner and extending to a point that intersects with the vertical crease made in step 9.

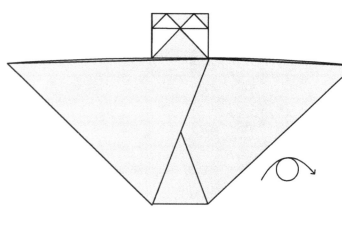

14. Turn the model over.

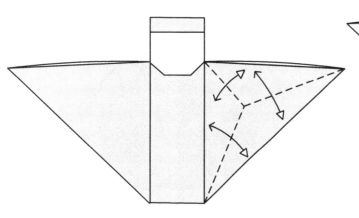

15. This step is precreasing only. Valley-fold and unfold each of the corners of the right flap in half, but only to the center.

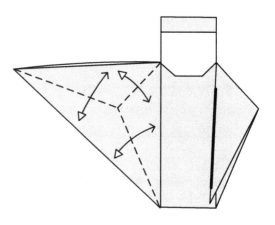

16. Pinch the top and lower right edges together (indicated with dark lines).

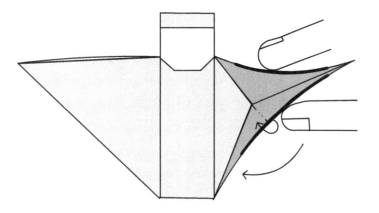

This continues the folding begun in step 16. Keep bringing all three corners together. Then lay the protruding flap down.

17. Repeat steps 15-16 on the left flap.

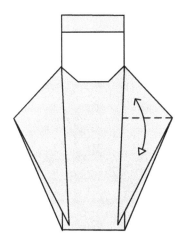

18. The next set of steps are done to make the arm. Valley-fold and unfold the flap on the right.

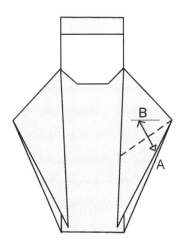

19. Valley-fold and unfold edge A to crease B, the one you made in step 18.

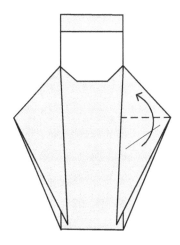

20. Valley-fold the flap up along the crease you made in step 18, and point it toward you.

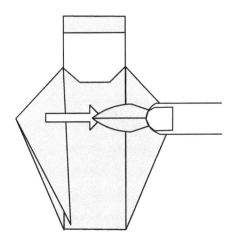

21. This is a 3-D view. While opening from the left, squash the arm flap down along the crease you made in step 19.

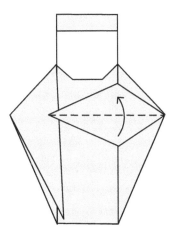

22. Fold the lower portion of the arm up along the existing horizontal crease.

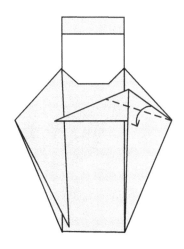

23. Valley-fold the top layer of the arm down, so that the upper right edge lies along the bottom of the arm.

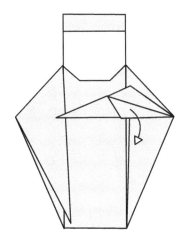

24. Unfold the crease made in step 22, without undoing the crease made in step 23.

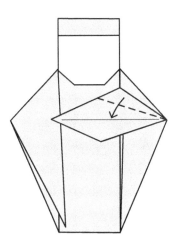

25. Valley-fold the top layer of the arm so that the edge lies along the center.

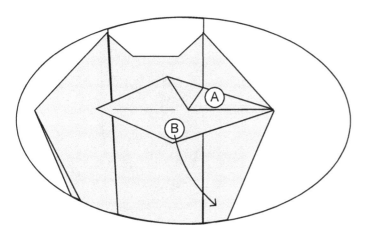

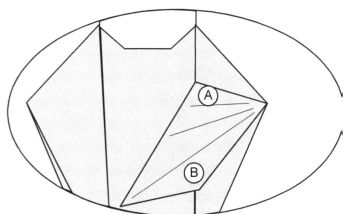

26. Gently press down at A. Now grasp all layers of the arm structure at B, and swing them down and to the right. While doing this, the layers under A move along with B. The top layer of A remains in place.

Here is the result of the move in step 26.

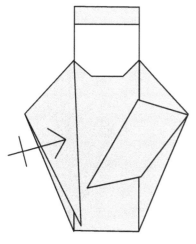

27. Repeat steps 18-26 with the flap on the left.

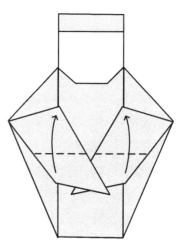

28. Valley-fold the arm flaps up along a crease parallel with the base of the model, and point them toward you so that they can hold a siddur.

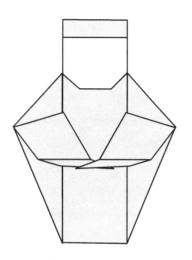

The Wise Son

The Wise Son Side View

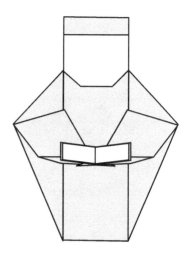

The Wise Son with Siddur

Wicked Son

Although he's better known as the Wicked Son, some translators have called him the Contrary Son. And that's how I've posed him—with his arms folded in defiance.

Begin with steps 1-6 of the Wise Son, page 44.

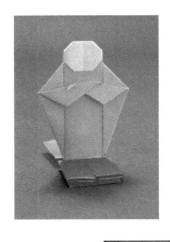

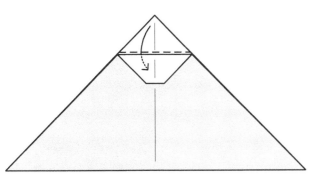

1. Valley-fold the top of the rear flap behind the front flap, with the edge flush with the top.

2. Turn the model over.

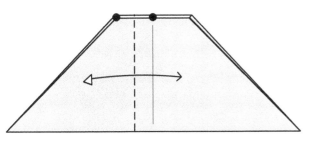

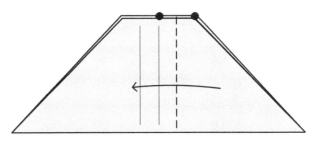

3. Bring the two dots together, creating a valley-fold that lies half-way between the upper left corner and the midpoint of the model. Then unfold.

4. Repeat step 3 on the right side, but do not unfold.

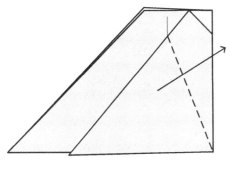

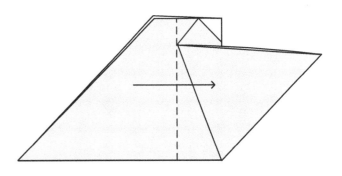

5. Valley-fold the flap, beginning at the lower right corner and extending to a point that intersects with the vertical crease made in step 3.

6. Valley-fold the left side over to the right using the crease made in step 3.

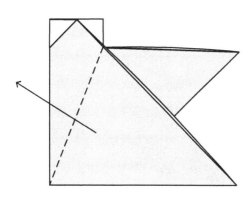

7. Valley fold the flap, beginning at the lower left corner and extending to a point that intersects with the vertical crease made in step 4.

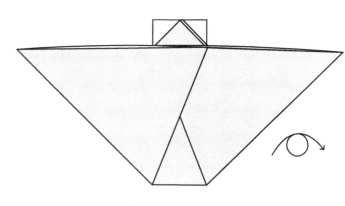

8. Turn the model over.

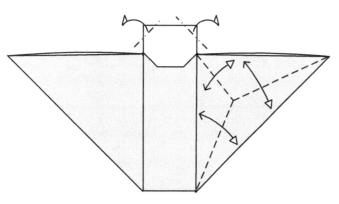

9. This step is precreasing only. Valley-fold and unfold each of the corners of the right flap in half, but only to the center. Then mountain-fold the left and right corners of the head behind.

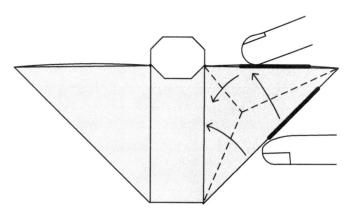

10. Pinch the top and lower right edges together (indicated with dark lines).

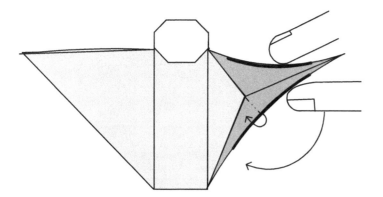

This continues the folding begun in step 10. Keep bringing all three corners together. Then lay the protruding flap down.

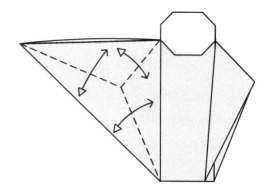

11. Repeat steps 9-10 on the left flap.

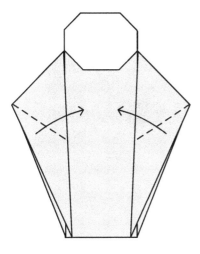

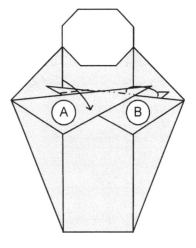

12. Valley-fold both arm flaps up so that they criss-cross, and their tips stick out a little above the opposite arms.

13. Mountain-fold the tip of arm A behind arm B. Valley-fold the tip of arm B on top of arm A.

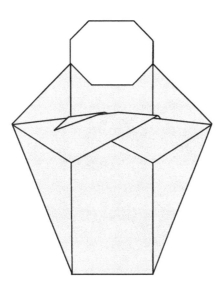

The Wicked (or Contrary) Son

Simple Son

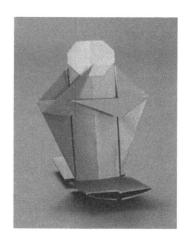

The Simple Son is a little slower than his wise and wicked brothers. He knows something important is going on, but doesn't quite know what. I show him with his arms in a gesture of pondering.

Begin with steps 1-6 of the Wise Son, page 44, and then steps 1-11 of the Wicked Son, page 49.

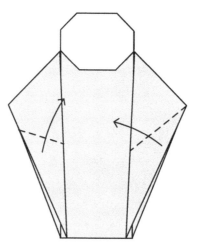

1. Valley-fold both arm flaps up, with the tip of the arm on the left under the chin, and the tip of the arm on the right supporting the other arm's elbow.

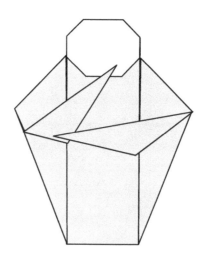

The Simple Son

Son Who Does Not Know How to Ask

The Son Who Does Not Know How to Ask hasn't yet acquired enough knowledge to even ask questions, so I've posed him with his arms in an "I don't know" gesture.

Begin with steps 1-6 of the Wise Son, page 44, and then steps 1-11 of the Wicked Son, page 49.

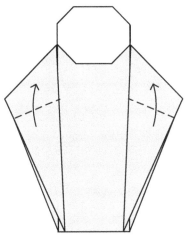

1. Valley-fold both arm flaps up and outward.

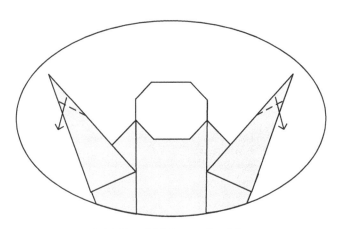

2. Valley-fold the ends of the arms down and outward.

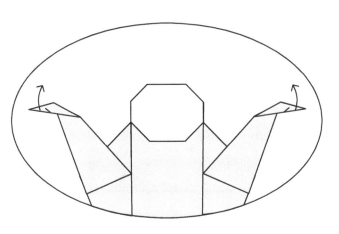

3. Valley-fold the tips of the hands up.

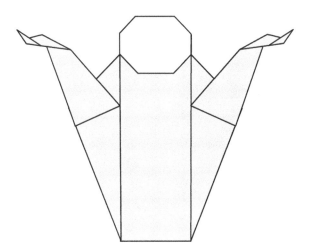

The Son Who Does Not Know How to Ask

Display Stand for Four Sons

This model enables the Four Sons to stand on their own. Make four of them, one for each son, using the same size paper as for the sons. The sons can then be easily displayed at your Seder table.

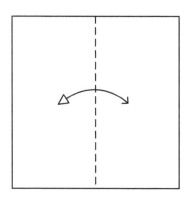

1. Begin with the white side facing you. Valley-fold the model in half left to right, then unfold.

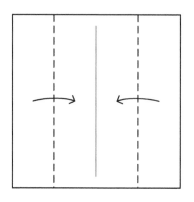

2. Valley-fold both right and left edges to the center.

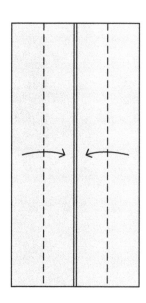

3. Valley-fold the long sides to the center again.

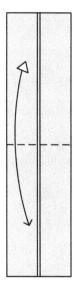

4. Valley-fold and unfold the top edge to the bottom.

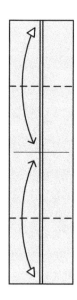

5. Valley-fold and unfold the top and bottom edges to the center.

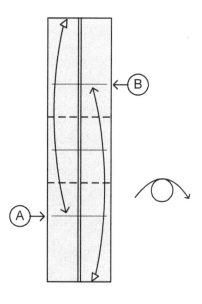

6. Valley-fold the top edge to crease A, then unfold. Valley-fold the bottom edge to crease B, then unfold. Turn the model over.

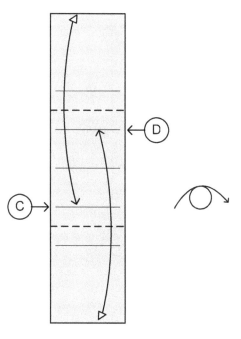

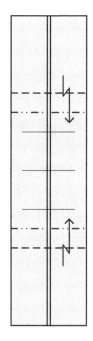

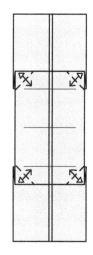

9. Valley-fold and unfold the four corners at 45° angles.

7. Valley-fold the top edge to crease C, then unfold. Valley-fold the bottom edge to crease D, then unfold. Turn the model over.

8. Using existing creases, pleat the top and bottom ends under the center rectangle.

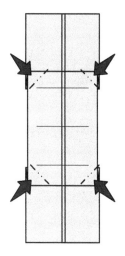

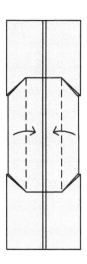

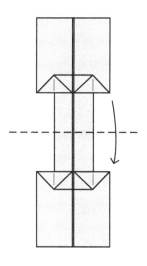

10. Push the four corners inside the model along the creases you made in step 9.

11. Valley-fold the long inside edges to the center.

12. Valley-fold the model in half, top to bottom.

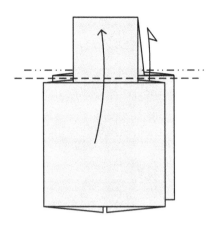

13. Valley-fold the front flap up so that it points outward toward you. Do the same with the back flap.

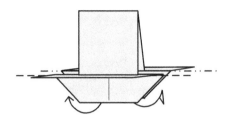

14. This is a 3-D view. Valley-fold the remaining trapezoidal flaps underneath up flush with the bottom.

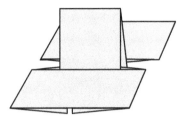

The Display Stand

Insert the protruding flap between the robe flaps in the back of the "son" figure.

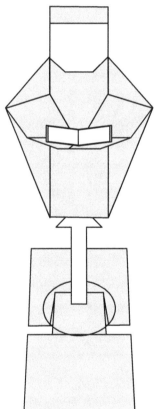

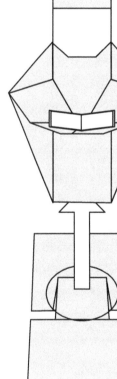

The Wise Son on the Display Stand

Sabbath Table

The Sabbath table is meant to remind us of the holy altar in the ancient Temple in Jerusalem. When we sprinkle salt on our challah, we reenact the way the sacrifices were offered there. When we speak words of Torah around our table, it becomes holy like the ancient altar.

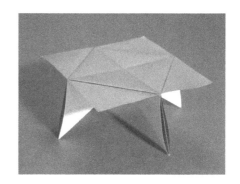

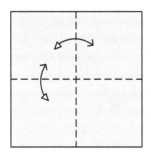

1. Begin with the color side up. Valley-fold and unfold the model side to side in both directions.

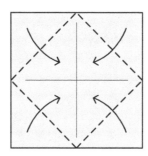

2. Valley-fold the four corners to the center.

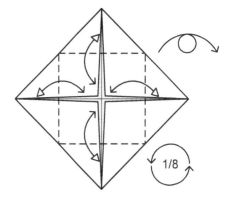

3. Valley-fold and unfold the four corners to the center. Then turn the model over and rotate it 1/8 of a turn.

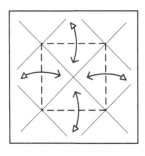

4. Valley-fold and unfold the four sides to the center, but only crease between the diagonals.

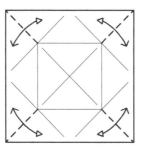

5. Valley-fold and unfold the four corners in half, but crease only as far as the corner of the center square.

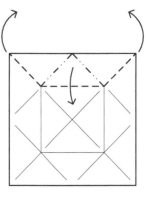

6. Valley-fold the mid-point of the top edge to the center. As you do this, the right and left corners will come up. The next drawing shows this step in progress.

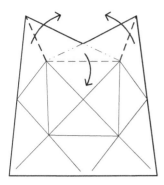

Step 6 in progress. This is a 3-D view. The triangles that are to be pressed together are shown shaded for clarity.

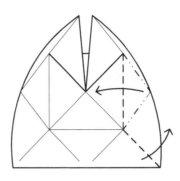

7. Valley-fold the mid-point of the right edge to the center.

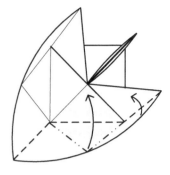

8. Valley-fold the mid-point of the bottom edge to the center.

9. Valley-fold the mid-point of the left edge to the center.

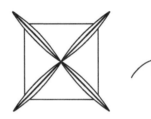

10. Turn the model over.

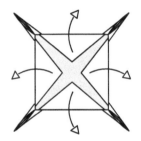

10. Unfold the four single-layer flaps from the center.

The Sabbath Table, from the top

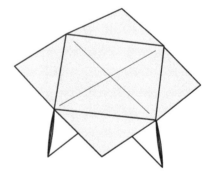

The Sabbath Table, another view

You can set up all four Sabbath models together as shown in this photo. The Siddur (page 7), Sabbath Candles (page 8), and Kiddush Cup (page 19) were each folded from a sheet of paper 1/9 the size of that used for the table. To divide a sheet into ninths, fold it into thirds in both directions.

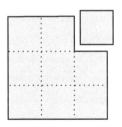

Torah Scroll

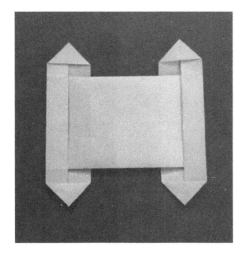

The word "Torah" refers both to the first five books of the Bible, as well as to all of Jewish learning. A Torah is made the same way today as in ancient times—the words are written with a quill on parchment that is rolled into a scroll.

This origami Torah is an action model, with two parts that can be pulled apart and pushed together, as if you are unrolling and rolling the scroll. The steps for both pieces are the same through step 12.

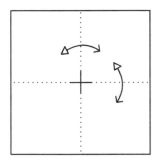

1. Begin with the white side up. Valley-fold side to side in both directions, but only pinch at the center.

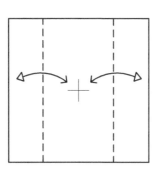

2. Valley-fold and unfold both sides to the center.

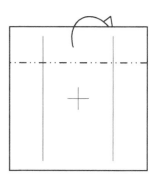

3. Mountain-fold the top edge to the center.

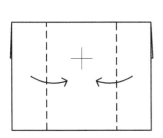

4. Refold the creases you made in step 2.

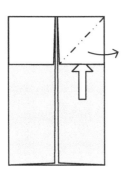

5. Insert your finger under the square flap at the upper right, and spread it open to the right. When it becomes triangular, squash it flat.

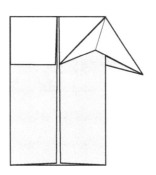

Step 5 in progress

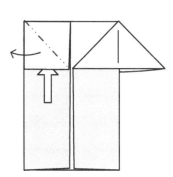

6. Repeat step 5 on the left side.

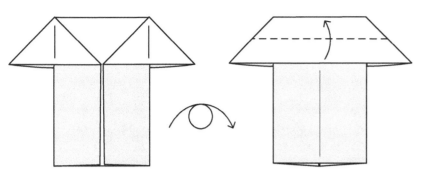

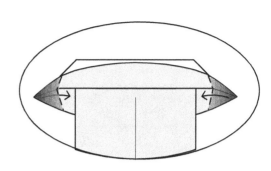

7. Turn the model over.

8. Valley-fold the bottom edge of the trapezoidal flap up to meet the top edge. As you do this, the corners on both sides curl up toward you.

9. Continue folding the edge to the top. As you go, the corners continue to curl toward you.

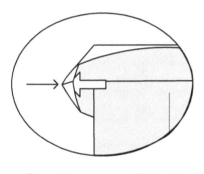

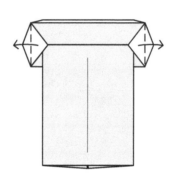

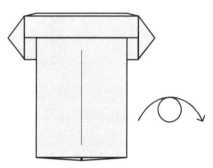

Step 9 in progress. This picture shows the left corner in 3-D. Insert your finger to hollow out the corner, then squash the flap flat. Do this on both sides.

10. Valley-fold the points of the two flaps outward at their widest points.

11. Turn the model over.

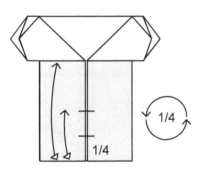

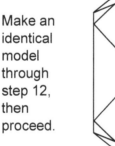

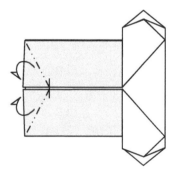

12. Locate the point 1/4 of the distance from the bottom of the colored square to its top. You can do this by first making a pinch at the half-way point, then another pinch at the quarter point. Then rotate the model 1/4 of a turn.

Make an identical model through step 12, then proceed.

13a. On the left piece, valley-fold the single layers along lines that connect the corners to the 1/4 pinch mark you made in step 12.

13b. On the right piece, mountain-fold (tuck under) the single layers along lines that connect the corners to the 1/4 pinch mark you made in step 12.

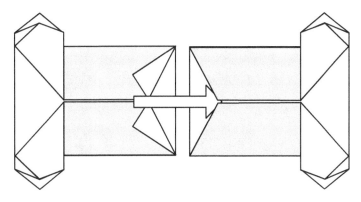

14. Feed the left piece into the right piece. The flaps you created in steps 13a and 13b form a lock that keeps the two halves from being pulled apart (if pulled gently).

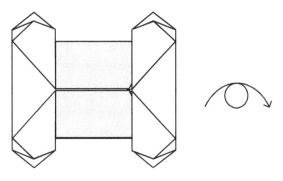

15. Turn the model over.

The two pieces can be pulled apart and pushed together. The lock works best with the model flat on the table.

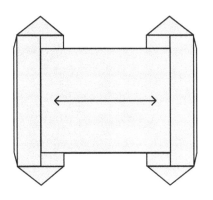

The Torah Scroll

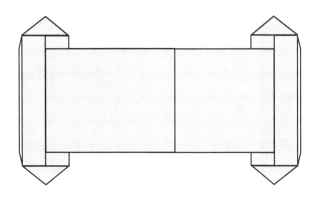

The Torah Scroll
Expanded

Megillah (Scroll of Esther)

The biblical book of Esther, also known as the "Megillah" or "scroll," tells how Queen Esther and her uncle Mordechai foiled the plot of the evil Haman to destroy the Jews of Persia. This victory is celebrated each year on the holiday of Purim.

We read the Megillah from a long piece of parchment, which often is housed in a cylindrical tube. As the words are chanted, the scroll is pulled out of the tube a little bit at a time. This origami Megillah is an action model, with a scroll that can be tucked in and pulled out.

Begin with steps 1-11 of the Torah, page 59.

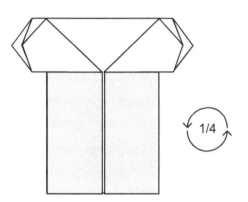

1. Rotate the model 1/4 turn counterclockwise.

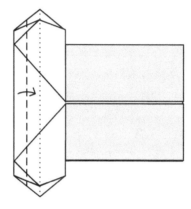

2. Valley-fold the left edge to lie along the center of the white section (indicated with a dotted line).

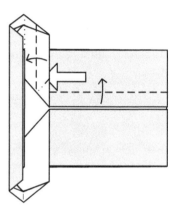

3. Valley-fold the right edge of the upper part of the white section to lie along the center (see the dotted line). As you do this, the horizontal part of the flap will curl up. Let it do so, then press it flat with a valley-fold.

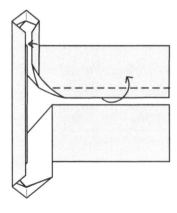

Step 3 in progress

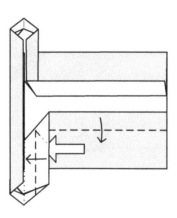

4. Step 3 completed. Repeat this maneuver on the lower flap.

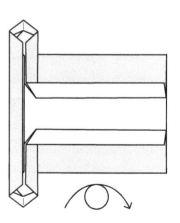

5. Turn the model over.

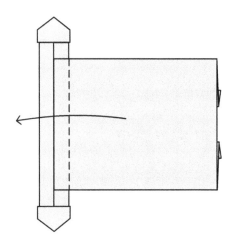

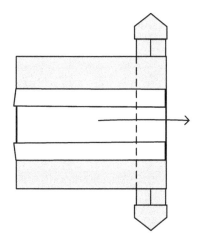

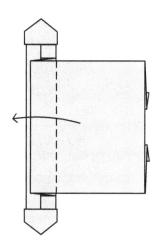

6. Valley-fold the rectangular part of the model, which we'll call the "scroll," to the left. The crease lies along the right edge of the underlying piece, which we'll call the "housing."

7. Valley-fold the scroll back over to the right, the crease aligning with the left edge of the housing.

8. Valley-fold the scroll to the left, again along the right edge of the housing.

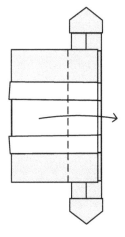

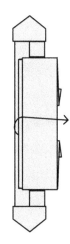

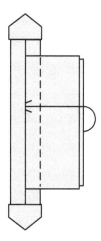

9. Valley-fold the scroll back over to the right, with the crease again aligning with the left edge of the housing.

10. Unfold the two layers of pleats to the right.

11. Valley-fold the two layers of pleats back to the left, tucking them into the pocket of the housing.

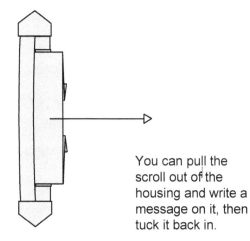

You can pull the scroll out of the housing and write a message on it, then tuck it back in.

The Megillah

Come to my
Purim Party!

The Megillah Expanded

Additional Resources

Origami Models
Books

There are hundreds of origami books available in many different languages. Here are a few in English geared toward beginning folders:

- *Jewish Origami, Jewish Origami II,* and *Bible Origami* by Florence Temko.
  Easy models on Jewish themes, written by a master origami teacher.

- *Teach Yourself Origami* by John Montroll.
  An excellent overview of the basics, with plenty of great models from simple to complex.

For reviews of many other origami books, see the "Book Reviews" section of Gilad Aharoni's Web site: www.giladorigami.com.

Web Sites

You can find just about anything you want to know about origami on the Internet. Here are two of the most popular and useful sites:

- *Origami Swami* – www.geocities.com/foldingca/swami.html
  A set of links to models from around the world, maintained by Dorothy Engleman. Excellent for beginners.

- *Joseph Wu Origami* – www.origami.as
  A rich catalog of origami information, including profiles of prominent folders and links to other sites.

Origami Paper

You can find origami paper at most art supply stores. Here are two sources on the Web:

- *Origami-USA* - www.origami-usa.org

- *Kim's Crane* - www.kimscrane.com

Origami Organizations

Below are the two largest origami organizations in the English-speaking world. On their Web sites you'll find lots of information, including listings of local area groups.

- *Origami-USA* - www.origami-usa.org

- *British Origami Society* - www.britishorigami.org.uk

Israel has two origami groups:

- *The Israeli Origami Center* - www.origami.co.il

- *The Israel Origami Art Society*, c/o Rosaly Yevnin, 24/633 Shachrai St., Jerusalem, Israel

Online Communities

There are two well-known listservs for origami:

- *Origami-L Listserv* – origami.kvi.nl
  The oldest online origami community, with searchable archives.

- *Origami-USA Forum* – ousa-members-subscribe@yahoogroups.com

---

About the Author

Joel Stern has enjoyed origami since his childhood. A native of Omaha, Nebraska, he has conducted many origami workshops in camps, schools, synagogues, and libraries. Joel is also the author of *Washington Pops!*, a collection of do-it-yourself pop-up cards of famous buildings in Washington, D.C. His origami and pop-up creations have been exhibited in the U.S. and Israel. Joel lives in Los Angeles with his wife Susan and their three children.